Published by Barbour Publishing, Inc., P.O. Box 719, Uhrichsville, Ohio 44683
http://www.barbourbooks.com

 Member of the
Evangelical Christian
Publishers Association

Printed in China.

HANG IN THERE

ELLYN SANNA

BARBOUR
PUBLISHING, INC.

Nothing great was ever done without much enduring.

CATHERINE OF SIENA

Contents

HANG IN THERE

1

You Have What It Takes

*(God has equipped you ahead of time to face every trial—
and He is with you no matter what.)*

*Y*ou will be strengthened with
his glorious power so that
you will have all the patience
and endurance you need.

COLOSSIANS 1:11 NLT

*E*ach of us may be sure that if God sends us
on stony paths, He will provide us with strong shoes,
and He will not send us out on any journey
for which He does not equip us well.

ALEXANDER MACLAREN

*G*od may be invisible, but He's in touch.
You may not be able to see Him,
but He is in control. . . .
That includes all of life—past, present, future.

CHARLES SWINDOLL

*G*od has not promised us an easy journey,
but He has promised us a safe journey.

WILLIAM C. MILLER

I know sometimes it feels as though life is just too hard. But I believe in you. I know the kind of person you are, and I know you can overcome even this.

God doesn't send us out into the battle unprepared; He gets us ready ahead of time, equipping us with the experiences and character and resources that we'll need. Sometimes we may think He's failed to do His job, though. Maybe that thought crossed David's mind when he was facing Goliath. After all, David was just a boy, without any armor, with only stones for weapons—and Goliath was a giant. But you know what happened to Goliath.

The same thing is going to happen to the giants in your life. So hang in there. Trust God—and believe in yourself. You're stronger than you think.

When you encounter difficulties and contradictions,
do not try to break them,
but bend them with gentleness and time.

FRANCIS DE SALES

Life is a pilgrimage, often from one need,
one problem, one solution to another.

MURIEL JAMES

Even when we try to run away from our troubles. . .
God will find us, bless us,
even when we feel most alone, unsure. . . .
God will find a way to let us know that He is
with us in this place, wherever we are.

KATHLEEN NORRIS

God is the God of promise.
He keeps His word,
even when that seems impossible,
even when the circumstances
seem to point to the opposite.

COLIN URQUHART

I wish I could bear this hard time for you.
I know I can't—but God can. And He is.
Even on the hardest, darkest days, He is with you.
I know sometimes you feel as though
He's forgotten all about you,
but He will never abandon you.
Neither will I.

But God has promised strength for the day,
rest for the labor, light for the way,
grace for the trials, help from above,
unfailing sympathy, undying love.

ANNIE JOHNSON FLINT

2

Things Will Be Better One Day

*(God has a purpose for every step of your path—
and He is leading you toward a brighter future.)*

*S*o be truly glad!
There is wonderful joy ahead,
even though the going is rough
for a while down here.

1 PETER 1:6 TLB

I know things are tough right now,
but just remember,
every flower that ever bloomed had to go
through a whole lot of dirt to get there!

BARBARA JOHNSON

S ometimes we have to let go of parts of ourselves before we can grow. It's as though life asks us to die a little bit—and dying is never fun. But think how tall and strong a garden grows when it's mulched with last year's plants; a garden yields a rich harvest when the soil is nourished with things that have died.

I believe God is doing the same in your life. It may seem as if too much in your life is dying—but if you just hang on, you'll find yourself growing because of these experiences. These tough times are the "mulch" that will one day nourish your soul.

E ndure and persist; this pain will turn to your good.

OVID

HANG IN THERE

$\mathcal{W}$hy not go out on a limb?
Isn't that where the fruit is?

FRANK SCULLY

$\mathcal{Y}$ou don't have to always play it safe. Safe may seem more comfortable—but sometimes, when we dare to venture out beyond our comfort zone, when we're sitting out there on that frail, bending bough with the wind tossing us back and forth, that's just the moment God drops the sweetest, brightest fruit into our hands.

Life is full of surprises. Don't give up now. You never know when suddenly, when you least expect it, you'll find that shiny fruit falling right into your hands.

HANG IN THERE

When you get into a tight place
and everything goes against you,
till it seems you could not hold on a minute longer,
never give up then;
for that is just the place and time
that the tide will turn.

HARRIET BEECHER STOWE

Be of good courage; all is before you,
and time passed in the difficult is never lost. . . .
What is required of us is that we love
the difficult and learn to deal with it.
In the difficult are the friendly forces,
the hands that work on us.

RAINER MARIA RILKE

We must accept finite disappointment,
but we must never lose infinite hope.

BARBARA JOHNSON

I have since learned that when
a baffling or painful experience comes,
the crucial thing is not always
to find the right answers,
but to ask the right questions. . . .
Often it is simply the right question at the right time
that propels us on into the journey of awakening.

SUE MONK KIDD

I know it's easier when you feel as though you have all the answers to your life. It's frightening when life seems to hold more questions than answers. But those times when we're confident we know it all, we're in control, we have all life's blanks neatly answered, and we're sure to get an A+. . .well, somehow, those aren't the times when we really grow.

Don't be afraid to ask questions. Remember what Jesus promised? He said, "Keep on asking, and you will be given what you ask for. Keep on looking, and you will find. Keep on knocking, and the door will be opened" (Matt. 7:7 NLT). So face your questions. Ask them honestly. And trust God to one day supply the answers that you need.

15

God possesses infinite knowledge and
an awareness which is uniquely His.
At all times, even in the midst of
any type of suffering,
I can realize that He knows, loves, watches,
understands, and more than that,
He has a purpose.

BILLY GRAHAM

Hang on. God will bring you through this time—
and when it's over you will shine like gold.
In the meantime, though,
please know I'm praying for you.
I know how painful the transformation
into gold can be.

Hold fast. However impossible it seems
that happiness and certainty will return—
they will, they will.
A thousand voices tell you so—
speaking from hard experience.

PAM BROWN

3

Look Toward the Light

*(A light lies at the end of even the longest tunnel—
and sometimes you may even find
some windows along the way.)*

*W*eeping may endure for a night,
but joy cometh in the morning.

PSALM 30:5 KJV

*W*hat does your anxiety do?
It does not empty tomorrow of its sorrow; but oh!
it empties today of its strength.

JAN MACLAREN

*H*ave courage for the great sorrows of life
and patience for the small ones;
and when you have laboriously accomplished
your daily task,
go to sleep in peace. God is awake.

VICTOR HUGO

*D*o not anticipate trouble
or worry about what may never happen.
Keep in the sunlight.

BENJAMIN FRANKLIN

Enjoy when you can,

and endure when you must.

GOETHE

Some troubles don't go away quickly.
But in the meantime my prayer for you is that
each day you'll find little things to enjoy—
the taste of food, a hot bath, a good book,
the sunshine on your face.
Even when life seems bleakest,
God sprinkles our lives with tiny treasures.
Be good to yourself, especially now.
Help yourself to these small pleasures.

HANG IN THERE

I got the blues thinking of the future,
so I left off and made some marmalade.
It's amazing how it cheers one to shred oranges
or scrub the floor.

D. H. LAWRENCE

*W*hen the world seems huge and dark and
meaningless, focus on little things—
sunlight through leaves,
a cat sprawled across your knees,
the taste of an apple, a dew-bright spider's web. . .
now is the time for gentle comforts,
for friendly and familiar things.

PAM BROWN

I think these difficult times have helped me to
understand better than before how infinitely rich
and beautiful life is in every way. . . .

ISAK DINESEN

20

*K*eep your face to the sunshine
and you cannot see the shadows.

HELEN KELLER

I know the way seems long and dark—
but I'm praying that God will help you focus on
the light that lies ahead instead of
the shadows that surround you.

*W*e fix our eyes not on what is seen,
but on what is unseen.
For what is seen is temporary,
but what is unseen is eternal.

2 CORINTHIANS 4:18 NIV

HANG IN THERE

$\mathcal{A}$ keen sense of humor helps us to
overlook the unbecoming, . . .
tolerate the unpleasant, overcome the unexpected,
and outlast the unbearable.

BILLY GRAHAM

$\mathcal{I}$ have seen what a laugh can do.
It can transform almost unbearable tears into
something bearable, even hopeful.

BOB HOPE

$\mathcal{I}$t is better to light a candle than to
curse the darkness.

ELEANOR ROOSEVELT

$\mathcal{N}$ever bear more than one trouble at a time.
Some people bear three kinds—
all they have had, all they have now,
and all they expect to have.

EDWARD EVERETT HALE

$\mathcal{D}$on't try to carry a heavier load than you have to.
Just deal with life one day at a time.
And don't forget to laugh sometimes.
Our burdens seem lighter when we smile.

$\mathcal{S}$ome there are that torment themselves afresh
with the memory of what is past;
others, again, afflict themselves with
apprehension of evils to come;
and very ridiculously both—
for the one does not now concern us,
and the other not yet. . . .
One should count each day a separate life.

SENCA

23

HANG IN THERE

I compare the troubles which we have to undergo in
the course of the year to a great bundle of fagots,
far too large for us to lift.
But God does not require us to carry
the whole at once.
He mercifully unties the bundle,
and gives us first one stick,
which we are to carry today, and then another,
which we are to carry tomorrow, and so on.
This we might easily manage,
if we would only take the burden
appointed for each day;
but we choose to increase our troubles by
carrying yesterday's stick over again today,
and adding tomorrow's burden to the load,
before we are required to bear it.

JOHN NEWTON

$\mathcal{A}$t day's end,
I turn all my problems over to God. . . .
He's going to be up anyway.

BARBARA JOHNSON

$\mathcal{T}$imes like these you need your sleep.
I hope you can make a practice every night
of letting your burden drop off
your shoulders into God's hands.
Try to relax.
You'll sleep better if you let God be
in charge of all that's worrying you.

$\mathcal{I}$ will lie down in peace and sleep,
for you alone, O LORD, will keep me safe.

PSALM 4:8 NLT

My prayer for you is that. . .

- you'll be able to catch a glimpse of the light that lies ahead of these dark days.
- you'll allow yourself time every day for something you enjoy.
- you'll find a reason to laugh at least once a day.
- you won't worry about the future or agonize over the past.
- at night you'll sleep well, knowing that God holds your life in His hands.

4

*Depend on
God's Strength*

*(God is always with you,
He always cares
and He's strong enough for even
the longest endurance race.)*

*M*y God is changeless in his love for me,
and he will come and help me.

PSALM 59:10 TLB

You have no strength but what God gives and you can have all the strength that God can give.

ANDREW MURRAY

The eternal God is your refuge, and underneath are the everlasting arms.

DEUTERONOMY 33:27 NIV

When we appeal to God as a helpless infant, He picks us up in His gentle hands and cradles us in His powerful arms. . . . [We] have nothing to lose by leaving it up to Him.

VINCENT P. COLLINS

$\mathcal{S}$ometimes it seems like we
can't go on a moment longer.
Our own strength is all used up,
and we feel as though we're falling into pieces.
Life is just too much for us to handle.
But it's okay to feel like that;
you don't have to be strong all the time.
Times like that you just have to let go—
and allow God the chance to take over.
His strength never fails.

$\mathcal{M}$y gracious favor is all you need.
My power works best in your weakness.

2 CORINTHIANS 12:9 NLT

HANG IN THERE

God cannot give us a happiness
and peace apart from Himself,
because it is not there.
There is no such thing.

C. S. LEWIS

Should we feel at times disheartened and
discouraged, a simple movement of
the heart toward God will renew. . .us.
He will give us at the moment the strength
and the courage that we need.

FRANCOIS FENELON

May. . .God our Father,
who loved us and by his grace gave us
eternal encouragement and good hope,
encourage your hearts and strengthen you
in every good deed and word.

2 THESSALONIANS 2:16–17 NIV

God has a thousand ways
Where I can see not one;
When all my means
have reached their end
Then His have just begun.

ESTHER GUYOT

No matter how dark and bumpy the ground may
be, we'd rather keep on our feet on the solid ground.
We want to walk on our own two feet;
we want to feel as though we're in control of our lives.
But God wants something else for us,
something that's terrifying. . .and wonderful.
He wants us to learn to fly.
That's my prayer for you today—
that you'll allow yourself to rest on God's wings.
Who knows how high He'll take you?

Those who wait on the LORD
will find new strength.
They will fly high on wings like eagles.

ISAIAH 40:31 NLT

32

Be like the bird that, halting in its flight
Awhile on boughs too slight,
Feels them give way beneath her,
and yet sings
Knowing that she hath wings.

VICTOR HUGO

*I*nstead of worrying, pray.
Let petitions and praises shape your worries into prayers,
letting God know your concerns.
Before you know it, a sense of God's wholeness,
everything coming together for good,
will come and settle you down.

PHILIPPIANS 4:6–7 THE MESSAGE

*B*e sure to remember that
nothing in your daily life is so insignificant
and so inconsequential that God will not help you
by answering your prayer.

OLE HALLESBY

I will refresh the weary and satisfy the faint.

JEREMIAH 31:25 NIV

I can tell you for an eternal truth
that troubled souls are always safe.
It is the untroubled that are in danger.
Trouble in itself is always a claim on love,
and God is love.
He must deny Himself if
He does not come to help the helpless.
It is the prisoners, and the blind, and the leper, and
the possessed, and the hungry, and the tempest-
tossed, who are His special care.
Therefore if you are lost and sick and bound,
you are just in the place where He can meet you.
Blessed are the mourners.
They shall be comforted.

ANDREW JUKES

HANG IN THERE

*Y*ou are leaving port under sealed orders
and in a troubled period.
You cannot know whither you are going
or what you are to do.
But why not take the Pilot on board who knows
the nature of your sealed orders from the outset
and who will shape your entire voyage accordingly?
He knows the shoals and the sandbanks,
the rocks and the reefs;
He will steer you safely into that celestial harbor
where your anchor will be cast for eternity.
Let His almighty nail-pierced hands
hold the wheel, and you will be safe.

PETER MARSHALL

5

Pass It On

*(Sometimes you'll find the most strength to endure
when you look beyond your own troubles
to another's need—
and God will bless you when
you share what He's given you.)*

Encourage each other and build each other up.

1 THESSALONIANS 5:11 NLT

No good work is ever done while
the heart is hot and anxious and fretted.

OLIVE SCHREINER

If you are unhappy with your lot in life,
build a service station on it.

CORRIE TEN BOOM

The true way of softening one's troubles is
to solace those of others.

MADAME DE MAINTENON

*External conditions are
the accidents of life.
The great enduring realities are
love and service.*

HELEN KELLER

No matter how tough your life
may seem right now,
you are important to the Kingdom of God.
You have so much to give—
so hang in there.
God is with you,
and He wants to use you for His glory.

$\mathcal{A}$ workable and effective way to meet
and overcome difficulties is
to take on someone else's problems.
It is a strange fact,
but you can often handle two difficulties—
your own and somebody else's—
better than you can handle your own alone.
That truth is based on a subtle law of self-giving
or outgoingness whereby you develop a
self-strengthening in the process.

NORMAN VINCENT PEALE

$\mathcal{T}$ he best cure for worry, depression, melancholy,
brooding, is to go deliberately forth and try to lift
with one's sympathy the gloom of somebody else.

ARNOLD BENNETT

HANG IN THERE